THE HISTORY OF
OPTICS

GILL LLOYD
AND
DAVID JEFFERIS

Thomson Learning
New York

CONTENTS

First published in the United States in 1995 by
Thomson Learning,
New York, NY

Published simultaneously in Great Britain by Wayland (Publishers) Ltd.

U.S. version copyright © 1995 Thomson Learning

U.K. version copyright © 1995 Wayland (Publishers) Ltd.

Library of Congress Cataloging-in-Publication Data
Lloyd, Gill.
    The history of optics / Gill Lloyd and David Jefferis.
        p.   cm.—(Science discovery)
    Includes bibliographical references and index.
    ISBN 1-56847-255-2
    1. Optics—History—Juvenile literature. 2. Optics—History—
Juvenile literature. [1. Optics—History.] I. Jefferis, David. II. Title.
III. Series: Science discovery (New York, N.Y.)
QC360.L56   1995
535'.09—dc20   95–4029

Printed in Italy

Acknowledgments
Concept David Jefferis
Text editor Michael Brown
Diagrams Robert and Rhoda Burns/Drawing Attention
Line illustrations James Robins
Cover design Norman Berger, New York

Picture credits
British Telecom plc. 40
Canon UK Ltd. 33
Delta Archive 4, 5, 6, 8, 10, 11, 14, 15, 18, 19, 20, 21, 22, 23(BR), 26(TL), 28, 29, 30, 31, 32, 34, 35, 43, 45, 46
Forestry Commission 9
NASA 16, 23
Philips Ltd. 15(TR)
Rod Williams/Bruce Coleman Ltd. 7
Science Photo Library 12, 13, 25, 26, 27, 44
U.S. Dept. of Energy 39
Cover: Splitting laser light with a prism; photograph provided by the New York Hall of Science, Flushing, New York; photo © 1992 Ken Howard.

☀ INTRODUCTION

Light is a form of energy that is so much a part of everyday life that it is easy to take for granted. The source of almost all natural light on our planet is the sun. The stars are glowing suns as well, and we see them because they glow with their own light; but the moons and planets of our solar system are visible only because they reflect light from the sun. Earth's moon is also visible because of reflection—moonlight is simply sunlight that has been reflected from the lunar surface.

Some of the simpler properties of light have been understood and used for thousands of years, while others have become apparent only after much scientific study. In this book we follow scientists in their search for an understanding of the nature of light and how to make use of it. The earliest of these optical explorers dealt with reflection, the ability of light to bounce off surfaces; and refraction, the apparent bending of light as it passes through one transparent substance to another (for example, from air to glass). Later researchers dealt with the nature of light—what it is and how fast it travels.

▶ Almost all natural light comes from the sun, almost 93 million miles away. Sunlight not only lets us see, but also provides the energy for all life on our planet.

 # THE SCIENCE OF OPTICS

Optics investigates what light is made of and how it is produced, transmitted, detected, measured, and used.

The sense of sight is something of a miracle. Everything we see comes through the lens of the eye as countless photons of light. Coating the inside of the eye's rear surface is a thin layer of tissue called the retina. Here, millions of light-sensitive cells are activated by the incoming light rays, transmitting the data as tiny electrical impulses that are passed along the optic nerve to the brain. Color, shape, size, and motion—all are analyzed and interpreted in the visual cortex and other parts of the brain in ways that scientists still do not fully understand. The result is a seamless vision of the world that we can use every waking moment, without even having to think about it.

Over the centuries, the study of light has led to some remarkable optical inventions, such as glassmaking. Although we don't know who made the first glass, an invaluable tool in optics, we do know that the Egyptians made glass beads and jewelry in 4000 B.C. Lenses and mirrors have been used to reflect and refract light and enable us to see far into space with telescopes. They also allow us to magnify tiny, nearly invisible objects with microscopes, to record light with cameras, and to project images in movie theaters and slide shows.

Optical development continues with devices such as the laser beam, optical fibers, and computers that use light beams instead of electric currents in their circuits.

◀ The pair of binoculars is just one of the countless optical tools used today.

LOOKING AT THE WORLD

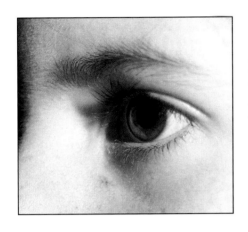

▲ The eye works by letting in light through a small hole called the pupil. The colored part around the pupil, the iris, is a ring of muscle that changes shape with the light. In dim light it opens up, enlarging the pupil to let in lots of light. In bright light the iris closes, letting in less light.

Eyes are our personal optical instruments. In ancient Greek times, some people believed that eyes sent out rays of light toward objects, illuminating them like the rays of a flashlight would. The Greeks thought that if something was put in front of the "eye-rays," it blocked their path and darkened the object. The Arab scientist Alhazen (965–1039), in about A.D. 1000, first suggested that vision worked the other way, that eyes take in light rather than give it out. His detailed examinations of the human eye formed the basis for a great deal of anatomical teaching and investigation.

In the seventeenth century, French philosopher and mathematician René Descartes (1596-1650) used simple geometrical diagrams to explain how light behaved when it entered the eye. He was able to describe how an image is focused on the retina at the back of the eye. Once the microscope was invented, scientists were able to observe how the retina sent messages to the brain.

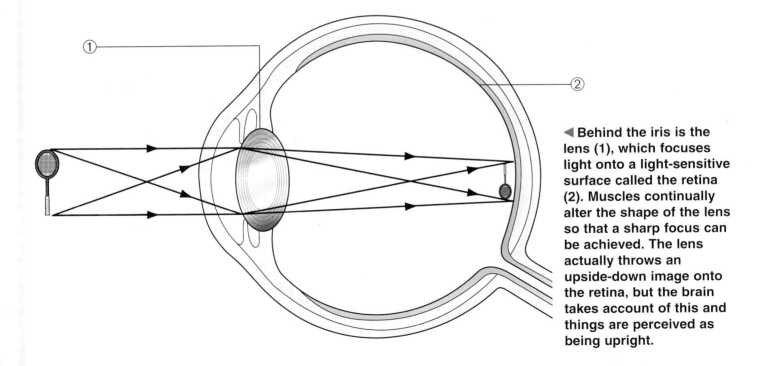

◀ Behind the iris is the lens (1), which focuses light onto a light-sensitive surface called the retina (2). Muscles continually alter the shape of the lens so that a sharp focus can be achieved. The lens actually throws an upside-down image onto the retina, but the brain takes account of this and things are perceived as being upright.

Most creatures have some ability to sense light. The simplest form is the flatworm's "eye spot," which can sense the difference between light and dark but cannot make out an actual image. Insects have eyes made up of hundreds of tiny compartments, each with its own lens. These compound eyes are very good at detecting movement but do not provide a sharp picture. Owls have large eyes with pupils that give good vision in dim light, for night hunting. They provide razor-sharp vision, necessary for this type of food-gathering. Cats, which also frequently hunt at night, have a layer of mirrorlike cells in their eyes that reflect whatever light there is—however little—onto the retina. If you see a cat's eyes shining in the dark, it is because light is being reflected from this layer, called the tapetum.

Humans have highly developed eyes, too. Our eyes are at the front of the head, facing forward. This allows us to get a wide view of our surroundings, which was most important when humans were evolving as hunting animals. Without good forward vision, a hunter will fail to see quarry and will not survive long. Each eye sees objects from a slightly different angle, which lets us judge depth and distance. This is called binocular vision and is something we share with various other hunters, including owls, cats, and dogs.

▲ Owls' eyes are specially adapted for night hunting. Huge pupils let in lots of light, while vision is incredibly sharp to allow owls to spot tiny prey—such as a mouse or a vole—from the air, even in the dark.

 RODS AND CONES

Rods and cones are the eye's light sensing cells, so-called for their different shapes. Cones specialize in bright light and color vision. They are concentrated in the central area of the retina. Rods are the more sensitive cells, but they are color-blind. They enable us to see even in dim light conditions, which explains why color vision fades as dusk turns to night.

☀ REFLECTING LIGHT

L ight travels in straight lines, which you can see simply by looking at a shaft of sunlight beaming to the ground. Shadows, too, are formed because light travels in straight lines. This was among the qualities of light that people found out about first—as early as 300 B.C., Greek mathematician Euclid wrote about the straight-line nature of light. He also wrote about reflection, the ability of light to bounce off objects.

There was not much progress in the study of optics until the upsurge of Arab science that started in the ninth century A.D. In the town of Basra, in what is now Iraq, the great scientist Alhazen carried out many experiments and compiled a work that became known as the *Optical Thesaurus*. In this he set out many of the basic laws of reflection, describing what happens to a ray of light when it strikes and bounces off flat and curved surfaces. He also dealt with refraction—the bending of light—and came remarkably close to grasping a working theory of magnification.

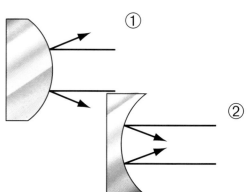

▲ A convex reflecting surface (1) bulges outward. When light rays strike this shape and are reflected, they spread out. The result is a wide-angle distorted image in which reflected objects look smaller than they actually are.

A concave surface (2) is one that dips inward. Reflected light rays converge when they bounce off such a mirror, resulting in a smaller, upside-down image. If you look from really close up, however, the image swings upright, but it is highly magnified.

◀ These spoons reflect images from the concave and convex surfaces.

When an incoming or "incident" ray hits a surface, an outgoing or "reflected" ray results. The reflected ray always returns at the same angle (the angle of incidence) as the incident ray, but on the opposite side of an imaginary line called the "normal," which stands at a right angle to the mirror surface.

Understanding an object in a mirror requires some mental gymnastics. Your brain actually sees reflected light, but it assumes that the rays have traveled in straight lines, which is why your mirror reflection looks back at you apparently from behind the mirror's surface. Such an image is called a virtual image because it does not produce or reflect light of its own. An image that does produce or reflect light of its own is called a real image.

▲ Shafts of sunlight on an autumn day clearly show the straight-line nature of light rays.

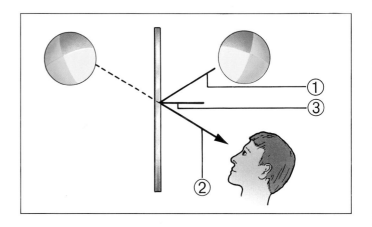

▲ Reflection involves two rays: the incoming incident ray (1) and the outgoing reflected ray (2). The two rays are at identical angles but on opposite sides of the normal (3). The virtual image appears to be behind the plane of the mirror.

REFRACTING LIGHT

When light rays pass from one substance to another, such as from air to glass, the rays are bent or refracted. You can see this effect by placing a straight stick into water at an angle. At the surface—which is the junction between the air and water—the stick looks bent. Refraction has been known about for as long as reflection has. Greek astronomer Ptolemy (A.D. 100-c.165) tried to develop a mathematical law to calculate the amount of bending that takes place. With some of his experiments he came very close to the answer, with measurements within half a degree of figures we would give today. Other calculations were less reliable, and it was not until Willebrord Snell's work in the 1600s that the laws of refraction were more precisely worked out.

▲ Willebrord Snell's pioneering experiments became the basis of much of the science of optics.

◀ This picture shows refraction in action. As the spoon passes through water, glass, and air, its image adopts different angles. The light rays are refracted at each junction between substances. You can see a similar effect if you look at underwater objects. Instead of looking at the actual object, the bent light rays make you see a virtual image that appears larger than the real thing.

The laws of refraction as understood today were worked out by Dutch mathematician and astronomer Willebrord Snell (1580-1626). In 1621, he discovered exactly what happened when light traveled from one transparent substance to another. For his experiment, Snell used a beam of light and a block of clear glass. He found that if the beam enters or leaves the block at 90° to the surface, it does not bend at all; but if it enters or leaves at any other angle, the amount of bending increases as the light beam veers away from the right angle position.

Snell proved that there was a definite relationship between a light beam's angle before being bent—its angle of incidence—and its angle after being bent—the angle of refraction. He also found out that every substance through which a beam of light passes has its own "bending power." He called this power the refractive index. Snell's work opened the door for much of today's applied optics.

 # ABSORBING LIGHT

Light can be reflected and refracted; it can also be absorbed and scattered as it passes through air and water. The setting sun often turns red as it nears the horizon because dust in the atmosphere scatters the green and blue light present in the sun's rays (see pages 12-13). This leaves just the red rays to come straight through the atmosphere. In the photograph below, the setting sun also has turned the clouds to shades of blood red.

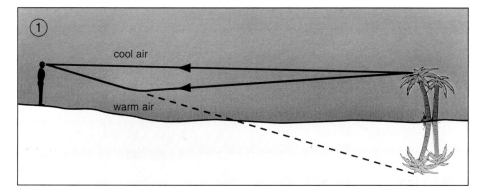

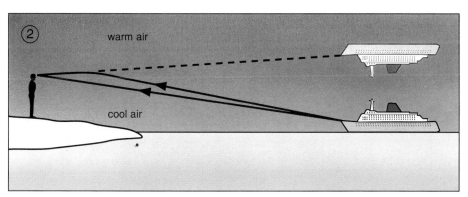

◀ One of the more spectacular effects of refraction is the mirage. Mirages are unusual in that light rays do not pass from one substance to another. Instead, layers of hot and cold air do the trick—cold air is denser than hot, so it has a different refractive index. A mirage (1) usually occurs when a layer of cool air traps warm air near the earth's surface. Light is refracted at the boundary between the two layers, resulting in an upside-down image. This type of mirage can be seen on roads in summer—what looks like a pool of water is actually a view of the sky.

A looming mirage (2) is caused by the opposite effect—warm air trapping a layer of cool air. The resulting mirage appears above the horizon.

☀ SPLITTING LIGHT

▲ Sir Isaac Newton (1642-1727) wrote two great scientific works, *Principia* (1687) and *Opticks* (1704), that have influenced scientists for centuries.

Since ancient times philosophers have been putting forward theories about the properties of color, but English scientist Sir Isaac Newton, whose experiments of 1665 revealed some of the secrets, was one of the earliest. As he explained, "I procured me a triangular glass prism to try therewith the celebrated phenomena of colors."

Newton performed an experiment in which he allowed a beam of sunlight to pass through a small slit in his window shutters and then into a prism. The prism split the white light into a range of different colors—the spectrum that we are familiar with today. Newton noticed that the prism bent different colors at different angles. He then passed just one of the colors through a second prism. The result? It stayed the same color, proving that while white light was made of different colors, these colors could not be split any further and single colors could not make white light. However, if a complete spectrum was aimed into a second prism, then white light came out the other side.

◀ You can perform Newton's experiment today simply by holding a glass prism in a beam of sunlight.

Looking at a rainbow is one of the easiest ways to see splitting light in nature, and Newton investigated this, too (though French philosopher René Descartes had also done some work before). Newton's prism experiments enabled him to understand that light refracting inside raindrops was what lay behind the rainbow's mystery. Man-made light-splitters include cut gems, such as diamonds. The facets act like a collection of prisms, each one specially cut and angled to cause the most glitter.

▶ **Rainbows occur because water refracts sunlight, splitting it into a spectrum. To see a rainbow the sun has to be behind you and rain or mist ahead.**

✳ THE VISIBLE SPECTRUM

The visible spectrum is the name given to the color range that we can see with unaided eyes. There are no hard junctions between the individual colors, but they are generally identified as red, orange, yellow, green, blue, indigo, and violet. The colors are refracted to varying degrees: red is bent the least, followed by the other shades all the way to violet, which is bent the most.

A WORLD OF COLOR

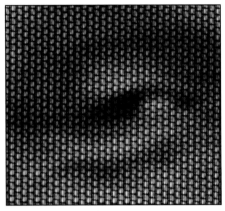

▲ Color television sets have RGB screens that use grids of tiny dots that glow red, green, and blue. Look closely and you can see the dots (on many TV sets they are short strips). Move back to viewing distance and they merge together to give a full-color television image.

Further experiments by Isaac Newton involved his color wheel. To make this apparatus, Newton painted the colors of the spectrum in pie-slice shapes on a flat disk. When it was spun fast enough, the individual colors disappeared—and, to the surprise of some people, blurred together to form dirty white. In fact, not all the colors are needed to do this—just red, green, and blue will produce white. These three colors are known as the additive primary colors; when they are added together in various combinations, they will make all the other colors, including white.

▶ One of the secondary colors—cyan, magenta, or yellow—is formed where a pair of primary colors overlap. Where all three primary colors overlap, white results, though you can see pure white only if the intensity of the three primaries is carefully balanced. When one or more colors is stronger than the others, the white will not be pure.

 The white of Newton's color wheel could never be perfectly clean because the dyes that made up the paints he used were not totally pure.

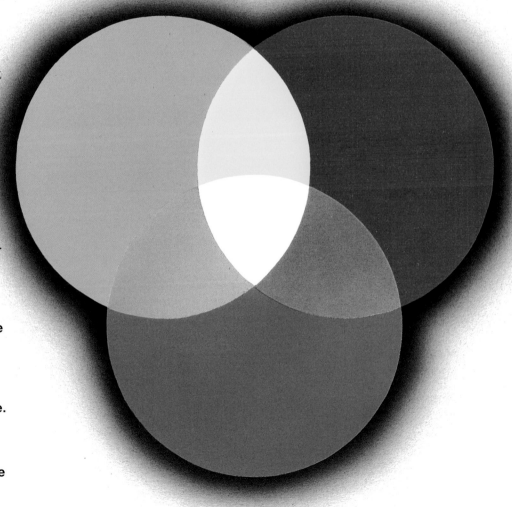

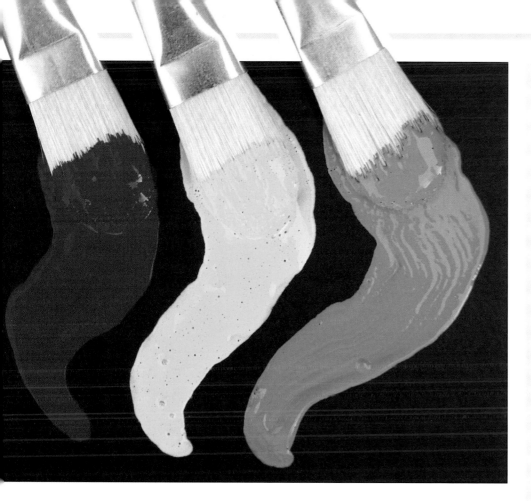

▲ The subtractive primary colors of cyan, magenta, and yellow can be mixed to make the color spectrum, but not white.

In practical terms, it is difficult to achieve a true black. Painters and printers usually add black as a separate color.

Additive color is made by things that produce their own light, whether it is the sun, a lightbulb, or a candle. Things that simply reflect light are colored by another process entirely, called color subtraction.

A primary subtractive color is what you get when you subtract one of the primary additive colors from the other additive colors. For example, when you subtract red light from white light, you are left with the additive colors green and blue, which make the color cyan. Subtracting blue leaves green and red, which make yellow. And subtracting green leaves blue and red, which make magenta. When the subtractive colors are printed, they reverse—so cyan becomes red, yellow becomes blue, and magenta becomes green. Mixing these three colors in various combinations creates all the other colors. Printers also use a special black ink to achieve intense dark areas. White cannot be mixed from inks, so on a printed page it is achieved by not printing on the white areas—the paper itself does the job.

WAVES OR PARTICLES?

Is light made of particles or waves? Until the eighteenth century, most people agreed with Newton's theory that light was made of particles.

In 1801 English physicist Thomas Young showed that in some ways light could travel like waves. When Young passed a light beam through a narrow slit, the light spread out, or "diffracted." If diffracting light waves crossed each other from slits close together, they formed either dark bands or bright fringes. Young likened this to waves in water, where some waves meet and cancel each other out, while others reinforce one another to create giant rollers.

The phenomenon was named interference. You can see it in action in the rainbow hues of a compact disc (shown above), the sheen of a pearl, iridescent peacock feathers, and the colors in a soap bubble. What these have in common is light that has been reflected from separate surfaces a tiny distance apart. Where the light waves interfere with each other, brilliant colors can be seen.

THE SPEED OF LIGHT

▲ Ole Romer measured the movement of Jupiter's moon, Io. By timing it at different points in its orbit, Romer could calculate the speed of light by measuring the moment of its appearance. He had a good stab at the answer, but his figure was some 50,000 miles per second too slow.

While scientists could argue about what light actually was, on one thing there was fairly general agreement – the speed of light was very fast indeed. The fact that light traveled at a definite speed was proved by Danish astronomer Ole Christensen Romer (1644-1710). Romer was making a careful study of Jupiter's moons and, in 1676, correctly predicted that Io, Jupiter's nearest moon, would emerge from the far side of the giant planet ten minutes later than other scientists expected. Romer predicted this because of the changing distance that light had to travel between Jupiter and Earth—the further away Io was, the longer its light would take to reach our planet. After careful calculation he figured the speed of light was 133,000 miles per second.

In the following century, many scientists tried to measure the speed of light more precisely, using apparatuses such as rotating wheels and mirrors. Frenchman Armand Fizeau (1819-1896) set up his experiments in the suburbs of Paris and was able to arrive at a speed of 196,000 miles per second, but it was not until 1926 that American physicist Albert Michelson made one of the first precise measurements. Today, the speed of light in a vacuum is known to be 186,282.3976 miles per second. Distances between stars are so vast that the distance light travels in a year—the light-year—has become the standard unit of distance in astronomy.

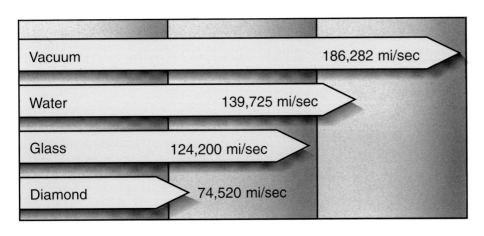

Vacuum	186,282 mi/sec
Water	139,725 mi/sec
Glass	124,200 mi/sec
Diamond	74,520 mi/sec

◀ According to Einstein's theory of relativity, the speed of light in a vacuum is the "speed limit" of the universe—it is possible to get very close to, but not to exceed, it. Yet light speed itself is not fixed; it varies as it passes through different substances, as the examples show.

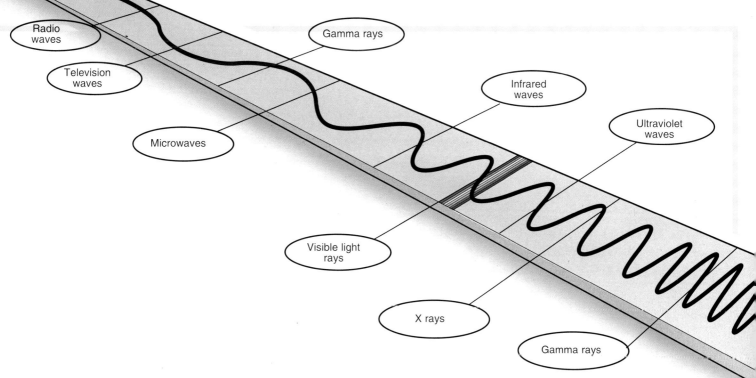

Radio waves

Television waves

Gamma rays

Microwaves

Infrared waves

Ultraviolet waves

Visible light rays

X rays

Gamma rays

L ong before the speed of light had been figured out, scientists were experimenting to find out if there were links between light and heat. In 1799, William Herschel discovered that warm objects glowed deep red while the hottest objects glowed blue-violet. But beyond either end of the color spectrum, he found readings where no light could be seen. He had discovered wavelengths on either side of the visible spectrum—our eyes cannot detect them.

Knowledge of light was also gained by studying electricity and magnetism. In 1845, British researcher Michael Faraday (1791-1867) established a link between electromagnetism and light when he found that the direction of a beam could be changed if a strong magnetic field was introduced. In 1864, Scottish physicist James Clerk Maxwell (1831-1879) predicted the existence of electromagnetic waves. He assumed that electric and magnetic fields acted together to produce radiant energy in the form of waves. His calculations proved that these waves radiated out from a source at exactly the speed of light. Maxwell died at the age of 48, eight years too soon to see the proof of his insights, which gave the wave theory of light a solid foundation. It was Heinrich Rudolph Hertz (1857-1894) who proved that light consisted of electromagnetic waves, by both generating and then detecting them. His work eventually led to today's understanding of the electromagnetic spectrum and so to the development of radio, television, and other electronic machines.

▲ Visible light is just a small part of the electromagnetic spectrum. Invisible radiation includes sunburn-inducing ultraviolet rays. Infrared is felt as heat, while X rays penetrate the soft parts of the body. X rays are used in hospitals to make photos that show breaks in bones. Gamma rays can pierce metal and concrete and can easily damage living cells. Microwaves and radio waves are used for cooking and communications.

HERO OF ALEXANDRIA

Hero, who lived in Alexandria in the first century A.D., was a Greek mathematician and physicist who demonstrated that the angle of reflection of light equaled the angle of incidence. He believed that light traveled instantaneously. This was considered true by the learned, except for a few like Alhazen, until the 17th century.

POLARIZATION

In 1669, Erasmus Bartholin (1625-1698) from Denmark made a unique discovery. In his notes of the time, he described how he saw a beam of light, passing through a transparent crystal called Iceland spar, split into two separate beams. If he held an object behind the spar, two images appeared within the crystal instead of one. Bartholin called this phenomenon double refraction and found that it occurs in some other crystals, such as mica and quartz. In 1808, French engineer Etienne-Louis Malus (1775-1812) noticed that one of the two refracted images disappeared if he looked at a crystal under reflected light. He decided that there must be two types of light involved, which behaved differently from each other. He coined the term *polarization* because each of the two types of light had to be of a different polarity from the other.

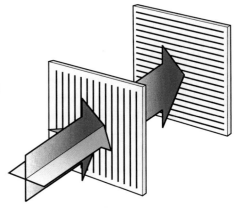

▲ Polarizing filters work by letting through light waves that vibrate in only one plane. Light can be darkened further or stopped completely by slowly rotating a second filter.

▶ Polaroid sunglassses developed from the principles of polarization.

 **Photographers often use a polarizing filter in front of the camera lens to make skies look more dramatic. A polarizer makes blue skies look darker and more intense, while leaving clouds white and fluffy. These pictures show the effect with a polarizing filter (left) and without one (above).**

Malus was right in his ideas. We now know that ordinary light is made up of waves that travel at all angles to the path of their light beam. Light that is polarized has been forced to travel in one plane only—up and down or from side to side, rather than in a mixture of all angles.

Light can be polarized by passing it through a filter that allows only waves that vibrate in one direction through, much like the slats of a venetian blind. If polarized light is passed through a second filter crossed at right angles to the first, no light at all gets through. Modern polaroid-type sunglasses are based on this principle. They were first developed by American inventor Edwin Herbert Land (of instant photography fame—see page 32), who devised polarized camera filters in 1934 to eliminate glare from surfaces such as glass and water. Polarized sunglasses are made with their filters set vertically to block the horizontally polarized light that reflects glaringly from such surfaces as snow, ice, or the sea.

✸TRANSLUCENCY

Just as polarizing filters can be used as light blockers, so other materials generally let light through in varying amounts. Glass and some minerals are transparent and let light through easily. Opaque materials let no light through, but may be transparent to other forms of radiation, such as X rays. Glass can be made translucent or almost opaque by mixing in small amounts of opaque materials such as metals. These scatter light, resulting in the misty appearance of the glass.

THE LENS

▲ The earliest eyeglasses were made to be held in the hand. Later a bridge was added between the lenses so that they could be worn on the nose, as shown here on a print dating back to the Middle Ages.

The idea of using glass to magnify objects or focus sunlight to a point goes back to ancient times. Glass objects and lenslike spheres, probably used for starting fires, have been found in Roman ruins. Roman philosopher Seneca (c. 4 B.C.-A.D. 65) pointed out that a glass globe filled with water could be used to magnify images. Emperor Nero watched battling gladiators while staring through a faceted jewel to help his vision. However, it was not until the late thirteenth century that glass lenses in the form of eyeglasses began to be worn. A Franciscan monk, Roger Bacon (c. 1220-1292), is often credited with the idea of using lenses for correcting poor vision, though no one knows for sure. Bacon also hinted at combining lenses to form a telescope. The first person to actually make a pair of glasses was probably a craftsman who was already making ornaments and glass for windows. Paintings depicting monks wearing eyeglasses appeared in the mid-1300s.

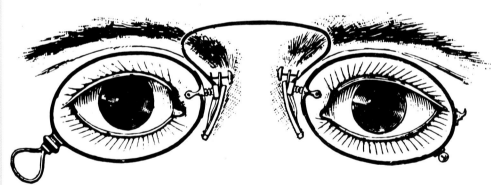

◀ These staring bespectacled eyes come from an advertisement printed in the late nineteenth century. Such illustrations were common in the sales catalogs of eyeglass-makers of the time. They were often used as signs, hung outside opticians' shops.

Franciscus Maurolycus (1494-1575) first published a work that put forward a theory of lenses as needed for correcting eyesight. He described light in terms of straight rays and suggested that the lens in the eye was similar to a glass lens. His theory about the correction of eyesight was that in a farsighted person, the lens of the eye had too small a curvature and a convex lens would be needed to correct the fault. In the nearsighted person, he figured, the lens is overly curved and refracts the light so much that a concave lens is necessary. This was remarkably close to a modern understanding of the problem.

The lens was so named for its resemblance to the small seeds of the lentil plant. The Italian for lens is *lente*, from the word *lenticchie*, or lentils. For more than three hundred years lenses were called glass lentils!

When people get older, their eye muscles weaken and it becomes increasingly difficult to focus well. The earliest glasses were convex lenses worn by farsighted people. Such people can see well when looking at objects far away, but when they try to focus on something close, their vision blurs. The convex lens cures this by focusing light on the retina. Nearsighted people suffer from myopia—close objects are sharp, but distant ones look blurred. Concave lenses can correct this condition. Of course, many people need correction for both far- and nearsightedness. In 1784, American scientist and statesman Benjamin Franklin invented bifocals, eyeglasses that cured both problems at the same time. Each lens is split into two sections—the top is used for distance vision, and the bottom is used for close work, such as reading or sewing.

 **CONTACT LENSES**

Contact lenses float on tears in the eye. They were first developed in 1887 by physician E. A. Fick in Switzerland. The first ones were big and clumsy, covering the white of the eye as well as the cornea. An American optician developed the much smaller corneal contact lens by accident—he was making a pair of the older type, when he broke off the outer part by mistake! Today's contact lenses are lightweight and made of plastic.

☀ EYES ON THE SKIES

▲ Apart from his astronomical discoveries, Galileo made many other observations, including the fact that a swinging pendulum could be used to measure time. He worked this out inside the cathedral in Pisa, Italy. A lamp was swinging from a cord and Galileo realized that it was taking the same time for each swing.

P eople have always been fascinated by the heavens, but observations could be made only with the naked eye until the early seventeenth century. In 1608, Hans Lippershey, a Dutch optician, made an optical device that used two convex lenses mounted at either end of a short tube—the first telescope—to focus light and make distant objects appear larger than a naked-eye view.

In Padua, Italy, mathematics professor Galileo Galilei (1564-1642) heard about Lippershey's invention and built his own instrument, carefully grinding the lenses to the right shape by hand. When he focused it on the moon, he discovered that its surface was mountainous and pitted. He illustrated his findings with sketches and published them in a newsletter called *Sidereus Nuncius* (Starry Messenger), which made him famous all over Europe. Galileo's best telescope, which magnified up to thirty times, worked on the principle of refracting light. A simple refracting telescope has two lenses. The front lens, called the objective lens, sits at one end of a long, narrow tube. It gathers light and focuses the image onto a second lens, the eyepiece, which actually magnifies the image.

◀ Galileo built several telescopes. Among his discoveries were Jupiter's four largest moons, which he spotted in 1610.

▶ One of Galileo's sketches of the moon's surface, as seen through the telescope. He made many such observations.

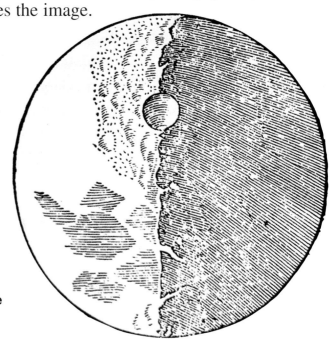

◀ This view of the moon, seen through the lens of a modern instrument, reveals in great detail the lunar mountains, valleys, and countless craters. Although the astronauts who flew the Apollo space missions of the 1960s and 1970s explored several areas of the moon, most of the moon's surface is unexplored to this day.

▼ These early brass binoculars are basically two refracting telescopes lined up side by side. Most modern binoculars are not straight-through designs like this, but use prisms to bend the light, allowing greater magnifications.

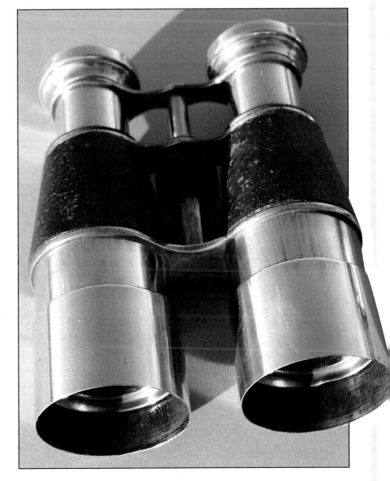

Galileo went on to make other important observations, such as the existence of the four biggest moons of Jupiter and that the Milky Way is made up of countless stars, most of them invisible to the naked eye. His observations convinced him that the system that had been proposed by Polish astronomer Nicholas Copernicus in 1543 was correct— that the earth and other planets travel around the sun. These findings were condemned by the Roman Catholic Church on the grounds that they opposed the teachings of the Bible, which were thought to imply that the Earth was the center of the universe.

Galileo was brought before the Inquisition and forced to renounce his views. He was sentenced to house arrest for his "dangerous" findings; but four years before his death, he smuggled out a book on mechanics and motion, which was published in Holland. The ideas in this book formed the basis for much modern physics.

GATHERING LIGHT

▲ Newton's reflecting telescope. This design helped solve a problem of refractors, chromatic aberration—color haloes around stars, caused by a lens being unable to focus all colors at the same point. More recent refractors use a type of lens that uses special glass to help solve the problem.

▼ These diagrams show the path light rays take in three popular types of telescopes. A refractor (shown at left) compared with a Newtonian reflector (center) and a Cassegrain reflector (right).

In 1668 Isaac Newton found a completely different way of making a telescope. He built an instrument that used mirrors instead of lenses. Newton's telescope used a small, flat mirror to reflect light from a primary curved mirror through an eyepiece on the side of the telescope tube. This first reflecting telescope was tiny—it was just six inches long and barely one inch across! Even so, through it Newton could see the moons of Jupiter, which Galileo had previously noted.

Newton's reflector showed that mirrors could be used successfully to magnify an image. It pioneered the way ahead in large instruments for other reasons, too. Large refractors have proved impractical, because the mass of a huge lens causes distortion in the glass and structural problems in mounting it firmly. Big mirrors are easier to support because they weigh less. They are also much easier and cheaper to make.

Early mirrors needed constant polishing because they were made of copper and tin, a mixture that tarnishes easily. In the mid-1800s, German chemist Justus von Liebig learned how to deposit a superthin coating of silver onto glass to produce a brilliant reflecting surface. Today, telescopes have glass mirrors coated with aluminum, which is even better than silver because it is cheaper and does not tarnish at all.

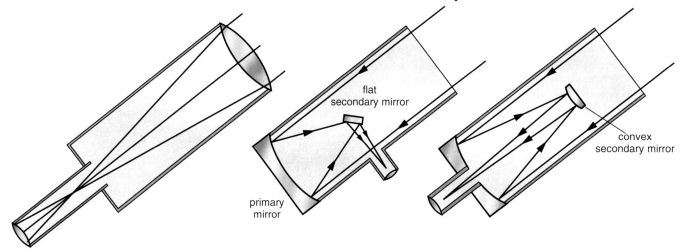

flat
secondary mirror

convex
secondary mirror

primary
mirror

The Keck telescope in Hawaii with a multiple-exposure view of the 1991 total eclipse of the sun

Another type of reflector often used today, especially by amateurs, is named after French physician N. Cassegrain. In 1672, Cassegrain designed a telescope that used a small convex mirror placed in front of the large primary mirror. The small mirror reflected light through a hole in the center of the primary mirror to an eyepiece located behind it. The Cassegrain's main advantage is that it can produce large images and high magnifications from a fairly short and compact instrument.

Telescope technology continues to develop, and there have been several recent breakthroughs. One new design is the segmented mirror used in the Keck Telescope on Hawaii. Completed in 1992, it consists of 36 hexagonal mirrors mounted close together. They are cheaper to make than one big one, with less distortion than would occur in a single mirror of this size. Powerful computers combine the multiple images into one picture. Another new development in lightweight mirror-making has been at the University of Arizona, where scientists are perfecting huge glass-honeycomb mirrors using a new technology known as spin-casting.

 **SPACE TELESCOPE**

The Hubble space telescope, an observatory that orbits Earth, was launched in 1990 from the Space Shuttle. It has a mirror eight feet wide. Early problems were solved during a 1994 manned space-repair mission; since then Hubble has produced superb images of distant space objects, from the planet Saturn to a galaxy 50 million light-years away. Hubble's vision is helped because it is far above the distorting effects of clouds, dust, and shifting air of Earth's atmosphere.

25

MICROSCOPES

If the telescope allowed people to explore the heavens, then the microscope revealed a world of tiny organisms that was just as mysterious. The idea of magnifying images seems to have arisen some 3,000 years ago. It is also thought that the ancient Romans may have used magnifying glasses made of rock crystal, while simple glass lenses were used in the late 1200s as magnifying instruments. However, about 1590, Dutch optician Zacharias Jansen (1588-1632) made a big breakthrough, when he combined two lenses to magnify and focus the image of an object. The principle of the modern compound microscope was born.

▲ This nineteenth-century microscope included such features as a mirror to help illuminate the specimen and a choice of lenses.

▶ Robert Hooke's careful drawings depicted a world of previously unknown detail to people of the seventeenth century.

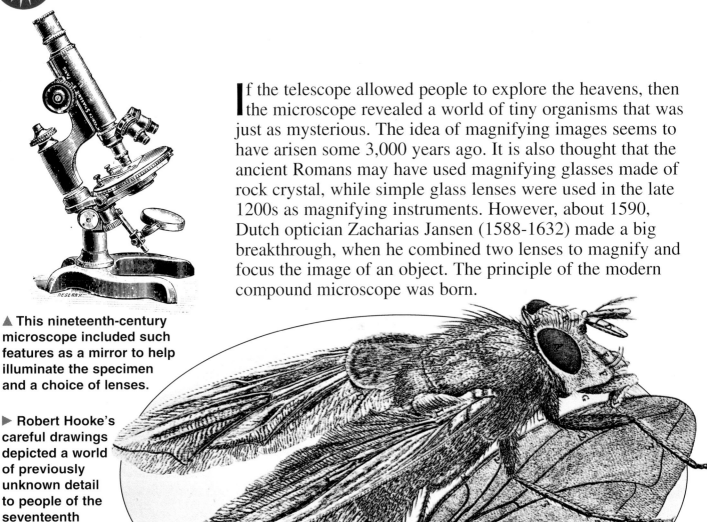

The first person to record observations of microscopic life was Dutch naturalist Antonie van Leeuwenhoek (1632-1723) of Delft, a cloth merchant by trade. He made his first microscopes to inspect the quality of the cloth he sold, but in 1674 Leeuwenhoek viewed tiny moving objects through his microscope and concluded that they were miniature creatures, which he called animalcules. They included what we now know as bacteria. Leeuwenhoek used a simple microscope for his pioneering work. This was a metal instrument with a single lens about $\frac{1}{4}$ inch thick, which could magnify up to 270 times. In order to look through the microscope, he held it up to his eye. The specimen being viewed was secured with a pin and moved back and forth by a screw rack to bring it into focus.

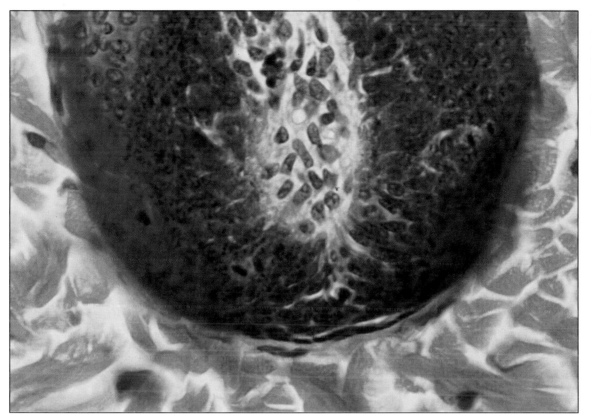

Robert Hooke (1635-1703), an Englishman, used the compound microscope to make some exciting discoveries. He made beautiful illustrations of his subjects in a book called *Micrographia*, revealing for the first time such secrets as the structure of the common flea and the barbs of a stinging nettle. He became curator of experiments for the Royal Society, the main scientific body in Great Britain and one that was world-renowned at the time.

The compound microscope used today has a number of lenses with different magnifying powers, set on a rotating turret. The specimen is placed on a glass slide, which is clipped into place. Cameras can be fitted to many microscopes, allowing photographs or videos to be made. Such microscopes can magnify up to 2,500 times. For higher magnifications, the electron microscope is used. This was invented independently in 1931 by two German scientists, Max Knoll and Ernst Ruska. It uses beams of electrons, rather than light rays, to form images, and its magnification power is hundreds of times stronger. Science, and medicine in particular, has been revolutionized by the electron microscope's ability to show things as small as viruses and even atomic structures.

☀ THE CURIOUS DUTCHMAN

Leeuwenhoek became a key figure in microscopy largely for his skill and curiosity. He was the first person to observe bacteria and investigated all manner of materials, from saliva and blood to cow dung and tooth scrapings. It was some two centuries before medical science caught up— Pasteur and other famous medical pioneers picked up where Leewenhoek left off.

Leeuwenhoek's microscope

RECORDING LIGHT

▲ The camera obscura (a Latin name for "dark chamber") was often used as a kind of peep show. People could sit inside, spying on the world outside. This one was built in the style of an ancient tower.

Greek philosopher Aristotle (384-322 B.C.) observed that light shining through a small hole in the wall of a room could project an upside-down image of the view outside if he held a white sheet in front of the hole. It was not until A.D. 1500 in Italy, however, that this observation was used for any practical purpose, with the development of the camera obscura. Early camera obscuras were room-sized, with seats so that people could sit and watch the world outside. Later camera obscuras were portable and were used by artists to trace the outline of a scene onto paper, forming an accurate basis for a painting. An artist who used this technique was the Italian painter Canaletto, who became famous for his detailed cityscapes of such places as Venice and London. By the 1660s, camera obscuras included lenses for crisp images and screens for viewing the results.

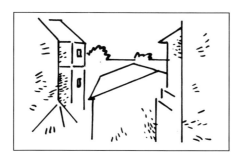

In 1727, German physicist Johann H. Schulze discovered that silver salts turned dark when exposed to light. Fifty years later, Carl Wilhelm Scheele (1742-1786), a Swedish chemist, showed that these changes could be made permanent if treated with certain chemicals. Finally, in 1826, photography became a reality when French inventor Joseph-Nicéphore Niepce (1765-1833) took the first photograph. He covered a pewter plate with a coating of light-sensitive bitumen and focused his camera obscura on a scene outside his studio window. After an eight-hour exposure, he rinsed the plate with chemicals, and the resulting photograph showed the view from his window. Although the image was fuzzy, it had been successfully recorded and permanently saved.

▲ Niepce's first picture: fuzzy, but still a landmark image. The small diagram outlines what is on the main image.

▶ A typical daguerreotype camera was made of wood, with brass trim. There was no button to press—a shutter was slid in front of the lens to one side. The back of the camera could be moved to focus the picture.

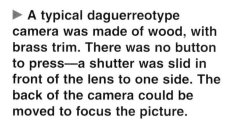

◀ Daguerre took this picture in the late 1830s. It includes one of the first persons ever to be photographed, a man having his shoes shined. The streets were not normally as empty as this, but only the man stayed in one place long enough for his image to be recorded. The exposure time for this shot was about five minutes.

▲ Louis Daguerre

The technique invented by Niepce was refined during the 1830s by a colleague of his, another French inventor named Louis Daguerre (1789-1851). After much experimenting, Daguerre treated a sheet of silver-coated copper with a more light-sensitive chemical and developed an image with mercury vapor, fixing it permanently with a salt solution. The first daguerreotypes, as Daguerre's pictures were called, required an exposure time of about half an hour, but they were excellent pictures. In 1839, the first daguerreotype cameras were produced for sale.

PHOTOGRAPHY DEVELOPS

About the same year that the daguerreotype was developed, British inventor William Henry Fox Talbot (1800-1877) invented a special type of light-sensitive paper. Using a camera made from a large box with a single lens, he placed his light-sensitive paper at the back and focused light on it for over an hour. The result of the exposure using his special material was not a normal-looking positive image, but a negative one in which light appeared black and dark appeared white.

Using this master negative in conjunction with a second recording session, Talbot could print endless positive paper prints. The prints were not quite as sharp as daguerreotypes, and the exposure time was longer, but the process of negative-to-positive transfer became the basis of modern photography. Being able to run off as many prints as were required was an overwhelming advantage.

▲ Talbot made his first negative when he was 35 years old. Talbot pioneered the method of photography that is most used today.

◄ ▼ Photography in the early days was a cumbersome business, requiring lots of equipment, as this picture of a traveling cameraman shows. Below, under the hood, an early photographer focuses his camera, preparing to shoot.

One of the biggest problems for the first photographers was the time needed to expose an image. The chemicals in early photographic emulsions were not very sensitive to light, so it could take many minutes to create an image—anything up to half an hour for an exposure was common. If anything happened to move during the exposure time, faint shadows would appear in the photograph, an effect known as ghosting. In fact, you can see the man's head and clothes ghosting in the daguerreotype on page 29. In 1840 Hungarian mathematician Joseph Petzval designed a special lens that gathered much more light than existing equipment. This reduced exposure times, making it easier to take pictures and to sit for them.

In the second half of the 1800s, scientists worked on improving cameras and processing techniques, but photographers required some skill in chemistry and the facility to process pictures immediately after taking them. They often traveled with wagons that served as mobile darkrooms and developing laboratories. In 1888, American George Eastman changed the whole nature of photography when he introduced the Kodak box camera, the first camera designed specifically for mass production and amateur use. It was cheap, light, and easy to handle, and photographers no longer had to process their own film. The Kodak used a roll of film that could hold up to 100 exposures. When finished, the film was returned, inside the unopened camera, to the Eastman Kodak company's plant in Rochester, New York, where it was taken out and processed. Prints were then made and returned to the customer. The company slogan was, "You press the button, we do the rest."

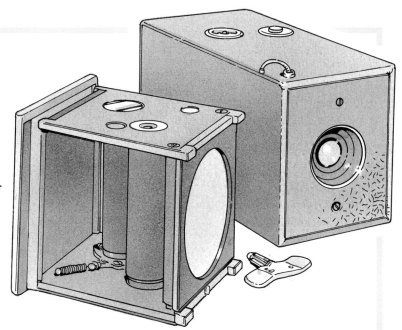

▲ Kodak's first point-and-shoot camera took up to 100 circular pictures at a time. The corners were trimmed off because the pictures had blurred edges.

▼ Later Kodak cameras had improved lenses and took normal square or rectangular photos. This one has a bellows so that it can be folded away when not in use.

MODERN CAMERAS

▲ These advertising images show the first Leica (top) and the first Rolleiflex. Both makes of camera are renowned for the superb optical quality of their lenses. All things being equal, the "Rollei" will provide better final prints because it uses a larger film format—so the negative does not have to be enlarged so much when making a print.

While the Kodak box camera made photography easy for millions, there was still a need for a small, versatile camera for serious photographers. This was invented in 1913 by Oskar Barnack (1879-1936), head of the experimental department at Germany's Leitz optical company. He called it the Leica I (from *Lei*tz *ca*mera) and launched it into the photographic world in 1924. Its design—small, easy to use, and able to take pictures in almost any conditions—has been a major influence on camera design since. In 1929 came the somewhat larger German Rolleiflex twin-lens reflex (it had one lens for viewing and one for picture-taking), and then, in 1937, the first single-lens reflex (SLR) camera.

In 1948 came the Polaroid Land Camera, invented by American engineer Edwin Land, that had chemicals built into the film cartridge allowing for on-the-spot print development. The early 1970s saw the Kodak Instamatic, with slip-in cartridge film for easy loading. Since then there have been many improvements in camera design: electronic cameras with central control units that operate shutter, exposure, flash, and focusing; compact cameras, pocket-sized and simple to use; zoom cameras with built-in zoom lenses; and single-use cameras, which are packaged with a roll of film already loaded, ready for picture-taking.

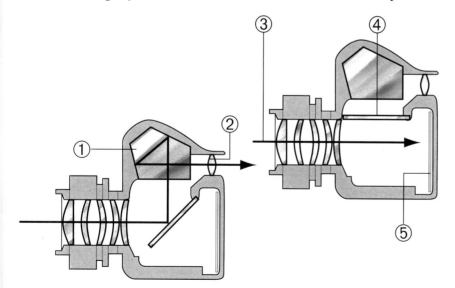

◀ The basic principle of even the most expensive camera remains that of a simple light box. Light reflects through a five-sided prism, or pentaprism (1), so that the photographer can view an upright image through the viewfinder (2). When the shutter clicks, light passes through a lens (3) and hits light-sensitive film inside the back of the camera body (5). This diagram shows how an SLR's mirror (4) snaps up to allow light to hit the film.

A top-quality modern SLR camera. Zoom lens, autofocus, and a pop-up flashgun are included in the list of standard features.

The most popular type of camera with professionals and serious amateurs is the 35-mm SLR. Compact and fairly lightweight, it produces high-quality images. Unlike the twin-lens reflex—where you look down at the viewfinder and see a reversed image—you hold an SLR at eye level, and what you see through the lens is what appears in the picture. When you press the release button to take a picture, a mirror inside the camera snaps up briefly to allow light to enter the lens and strike the film.

The SLR is very versatile; you can remove the lens and replace it with an assortment of alternatives. These may include a fish-eye lens (making a super-wide, distorted picture), a wide-angle lens, a telephoto lens, a zoom lens, or a macro lens for close-up photography. The telephoto lens was the first of these to have been invented, in 1891, from a design by John Henry Dallmeyer (1830-1883), a German optician who came to live in London in 1851. The zoom lens was invented by the Austrian firm of Voigtlander in 1959.

 ## STEREOSCOPIC PICTURES

A popular device of the nineteenth century was the stereoscope, found in almost every home across Europe and the United States. Invented in 1832 by Englishman Sir Charles Wheatstone, it was a twin-lens device with which were viewed a pair of pictures to give a 3-D image. It relied on the fact that each eye sees a slightly different view of the same scene, and the brain merges the two views to give a single image with the illusion of depth. By the 1870s, millions of double-image photo cards had been sold, showing all kinds of subjects, including famous sights such as the pyramids of Egypt and ancient Greek ruins.

In the 1940s and 1950s, a new stereo device became popular—the View-Master, launched by the Sawyer firm in Oregon. It consisted of a plastic viewer and disks of small, colored pictures set in a circular card. By pressing a lever on the viewer, you could move the paired pictures from scene to scene. In the 1990s, 3-D has been revived by ImageTech of the United States, whose cameras produce photos that need no special viewer for a person to see the 3-D effect.

MAGIC LANTERNS TO MOVIES

The magic lantern is thought to have been invented in Germany by Athanasius Kircher in 1646. It was a device for projecting colored pictures painted on glass slides onto a screen. By the nineteenth century, magic lantern shows were very popular and were the archetypes of the motion pictures we know today. The advance toward moving pictures really gathered speed after 1824, when researchers found that the brain retains an image for a fraction of a second longer than it is actually seen and blends that image with the next one. Many gadgets were invented to take advantage of this phenomenon. One of them was the zoetrope, a slotted drum lined with pictures of clowns, acrobats, or horses. As the drum was spun around, each picture could be seen for a moment through a slot. If the zoetrope was rotated fast enough, the images gave the illusion of movement.

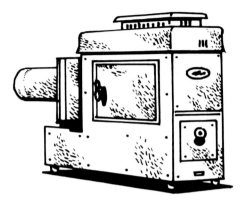

▲ A magic lantern of the 1800s, made to project pictures painted on transparent slides. A relative of the magic lantern was the epidiascope, which used a mirror system to project pictures laid flat under the machine's base.

▲ One of Muybridge's famous photo sequences. His sequences showed a succession of images, but they were not made as movies.

Eadweard Muybridge (1830-1904), a British photographer, took the first successful pictures showing movement in 1877, when he was commissioned by Governor Leland Stanford of California to take pictures of his favorite racehorse galloping. Muybridge set up a row of twelve cameras with strings attached to their shutters. When the horse ran by it broke each string in turn, tripping the shutters and producing a succession of photographs. The result was a series of pictures showing how the horse moved, which caused lots of interest because no one had seen an animal frozen in midstride before. The action of the four legs was different from what had been thought. By 1899, Muybridge's experiments in capturing action had come to the attention of famous American inventor Thomas Alva Edison (1847-1931). Edison met Muybridge and was very impressed by the Englishman's zoopraxiscope, which projected drawings of his animal action photographs.

Movie film was perfected by George Eastman in 1888. The material, a type of plastic called celluloid, had to be strong and flexible enough to take the strain of being pulled through a camera or projector. In 1890 Thomas Edison's assistant, W.K.L. Dickson (1860-1935), devised a way of moving this new roll film. It was pulled by a metal claw, each frame pausing briefly behind the lens for exposure before being wound on. While each frame paused, a light projected its image at a screen.

The way was now open for the birth of the movies as we know them, and a few years later two French brothers, Auguste and Louis Lumière, pioneered the way forward with their Cinematographe, a machine that both took and projected moving pictures. For screening, a powerful light shone through a filmstrip printed with hundreds of frames that had been exposed beforehand. The Lumière brothers' first film, shown publicly in Paris in 1895, marked a historic moment and is regarded as the dawn of the movie industry. Though these early films were flickery and silent, the craze to see them boomed and soon hundreds of theaters were showing the new "moving" pictures.

PERSISTENCE OF VISION

The optical illusion known as persistence of vision is what makes movies possible. If a picture is shown for a fraction of a second, the brain retains that image and blends it smoothly with succeeding images, creating the illusion of movement. Early projectors ran at about 16 frames per second (fps), just fast enough to give the impression of movement. Today's projectors run movies at 24 fps for smoother results, while television programs run at 25 fps.

OPTICAL ILLUSIONS

The motion picture is not the only optical illusion that we come across—persistence of vision makes fluorescent lighting possible, for instance, because such lights flicker about 60 times a second, far too fast for most people to notice. In fact, the brain can be fooled by all sorts of other visual tricks, some of which are shown on these pages. Luckily, we do not normally come across illusions as strong as these in daily life, because there are usually multiple visual clues around us to help our brains interpret what is going on. Most of these illusions work largely because the images have been simplified—the brain is given very little information to work with, so it has to play guessing games.

▲ The illusion of movement is one of the most useful of all, as anyone watching a movie or the television can confirm. This machine, a tachistoscope of the 1890s, was one of many that produced a "moving" image.

▶ Check out your blind spot with this diagram. Cover your right eye and stare at the cross. Move closer to the page and notice how the red dot disappears when you are a short distance away. This is because at this point the image is focused on the blind spot, which has no vision sensors. The interesting thing is that you do not see a blank hole—the brain fills in the gap with detail from adjoining areas, which is why we don't normally notice the problem.

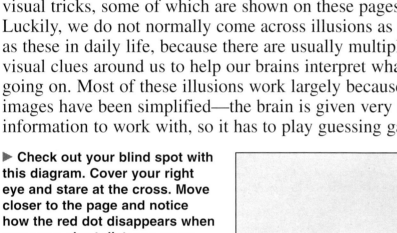

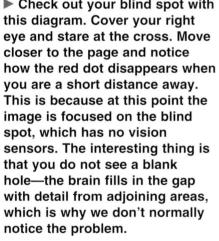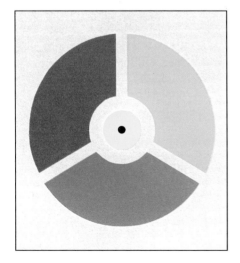

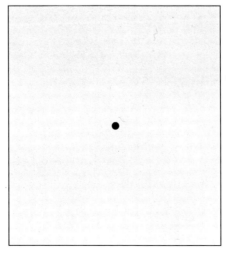

◀ You can view afterimages at work. Stare at the dot at the center of the color pie for a minute, then gaze at the dot on the blank panel. The pie appears in ghostly afterimage form, but the colors are in complementary, or reverse, order. Red appears green, yellow is blue, blue is yellow, and green looks red. Why this occurs is not yet completely understood, but it is thought to be connected with the eye's color receptors getting fatigued by overexposure to a single stimulus.

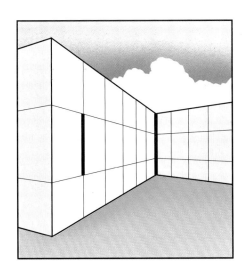

◀ Perspective can play big tricks on the mind. Here, the brain instantly perceives the "near" line as being the shorter one. Measure the two thick lines and you will find they are actually the same length.

◀ Light and shade play a big part in our perception of the world. We automatically assume light comes from above, with shade below. Rotate this picture left to see domes; turn it right to see craters.

▶ Color vision can be mysterious. Here the two grays are actually the same color, yet they usually appear darker and lighter, because the brain compensates for the large color areas behind.

◀ Parts of the brain that are used for angle and orientation can be fooled. Here, lines are made to look bent by adding short cross-strokes. Look closely from the bottom right and you will see they are parallel.

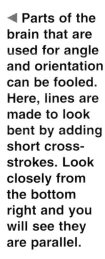

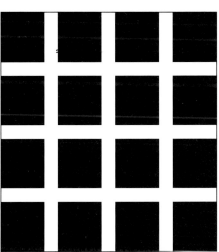

◀ Gray spots shimmer in the corners by the squares. The eye cells of the retina under- or overrespond to the high contrast of the black-and-white scene, creating a midway visual response in the junctions.

 ## SUPERMARKET ILLUSIONS

The art of illusion does not end with puzzles like the ones on these pages. Knowledge of how our perceptions can be fooled (or at least modified) is used by many commercial companies, not least by supermarket managers, who wish to make shopping more comfortable for their shoppers and, of course, boost sales as well.

Color can be used to produce various reactions in customers—cool blues can be used at fish counters, for example, to suggest an atmosphere of freshness and the sea. Crisp greens are often used at vegetable displays.

Bright spotlighting and brilliant colors can be used to boost sales of high-value goods (which are often displayed at eye level to make them more noticeable), while cheaper items are consigned to the poorly lit bottom areas of the shelves.

Mirrors are widely used and are good illusion creators: not only can they be used to apparently increase the size of the store itself, but can create a message of superabundance. The hidden message is that all you want is right here.

The persuaders of the commercial world do not stop with optical illusions, either—some stores have been known to pump an enticing "authentic" fresh-bread aroma out into the parking lot!

THE LASER BEAM

The laser is one of the most recent optical inventions. It is a machine that emits an intense light beam that is different in several ways from ordinary light. The rays in a laser beam travel almost in parallel, so that the beam does not spread out quickly. A high-power laser aimed at the moon, about 238,900 miles distant, will be only a few hundred yards across when it hits the lunar surface. Laser light rays are the same color (all red or all green, for instance), unlike ordinary light, which is a mixture. And laser light is coherent—the rays move in step, like marching troops. Because of these three qualities, laser light packs more energy, size for size, than any other light source.

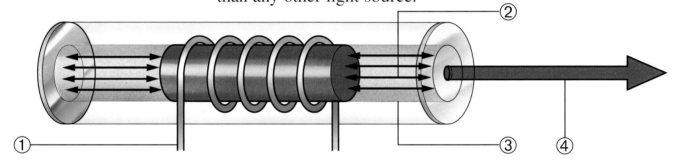

▲ A laser can have a gas, liquid, or solid as a working medium; examples include ruby (a solid) and argon (a gas). They work in a similar way. A power supply (1) pumps in energy, exciting the atoms of the medium to release light. As the energy increases, light (2) bounces off each end of the laser tube (3), until enough energy is available to emerge as a laser beam (4). The word itself comes from the words *L*ight *A*mplification by the *S*timulated *E*mission of *R*adiation.

The dawn of the laser lies in scientific work carried out between 1910 and 1920, when some scientists, including Albert Einstein (1879-1955), realized that atoms could be made to emit light of just one wavelength if enough energy was fed into them. This understanding led to the theory of laser emission, first suggested in 1957 by American scientist Arthur Schawlow. Three years later Theodore Maiman (b. 1927) built the first laser at the Hughes Laboratory in Malibu, California. It was a ruby laser, which produced a vivid red beam. To create it, Maiman took a pencil-sized rod of ruby crystal and put it into a cylinder with mirrors at either end. Around the cylinder he wrapped a powerful flash tube to pump in the energy required. When this gave off a flash, the ruby crystal's atoms became excited, giving off bursts of light that bounced back and forth between the mirrors. Soon, enough energy had been absorbed from the flash tube for ruby light to burst out of one end of the cylinder as a torrent of coherent light—the world's first laser beam.

At first the laser was little more than a scientific curiosity, but soon ideas for using it started to roll in and now lasers are used for a host of jobs, from the intensely powerful beam that can burn through steel plate to the delicate helium-neon laser that can be used to weld a detached retina back into place on an eyeball.

Lasers can also be used to make 3-D pictures called holograms. The basic idea was developed in 1947 by Hungarian-born British physicist Dennis Gabor (1900-1979), but only became practicable after the laser had been invented. A hologram is recorded by splitting a laser beam: one half goes straight to a photographic plate; the other is reflected off the object being recorded and then onto the plate. The two beams interact on the plate, creating a pattern in the film that contains information about the object. When the plate is exposed and developed, the original object appears to float within the photographic plate. If you move your head, you can see around it, as if it were really there. There are various kinds of holograms. Some can be seen only by laser light, while others can be seen in ordinary light. Holograms are almost impossible to copy, so many companies use them on important documents such as credit cards to avoid forgeries. They are also useful for recording art objects for archival purposes and recordkeeping.

▲ This laser is used for drilling steel plate. Unlike a conventional tool, the laser does not need sharpening or cooling.

 AN OPTICAL FUTURE

A far-reaching revolution in the communications industry is quietly taking place. A group of emerging information technologies is being developed that rely on the transmission of information using light beams that pass along fiber optic cables. Ultimately every movie, every piece of music, and every book ever produced could be available on demand, together with an almost infinite amount of reference information, on this optical superhighway.

The principle of fiber optics, light-pipes that can transmit light through fibers of glass or plastic, was discovered as long ago as 1927 by British scientist John Logie Baird. The first ones were made by Narinder Kapary in 1955 in London. Optical fibers are made up of two parts—an inner core and an outer covering or cladding. The core is made of a transparent material, such as glass or plastic, which allows light to pass through easily. The cladding is made of a material that reflects or bends light rays inward. Light travels through the fiber in a zigzag pattern, which, because it cannot escape except at the ends, is called total internal reflection. It is not unique to optical fibers, however—the pentaprism used in binoculars and SLR cameras uses the same qualities of reflection. Optical fiber links are now being laid all over the world.

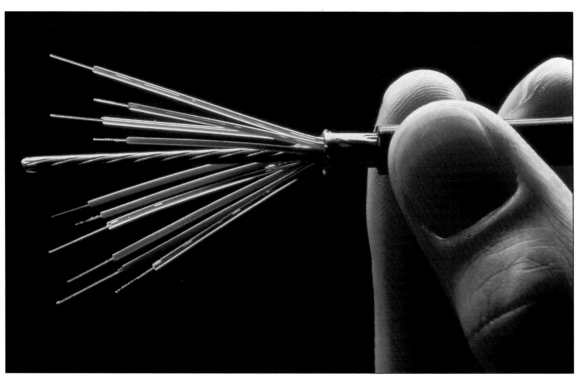

◀ A bunch of optical fibers. Each one can transmit about 32,000 times as much information as the equivalent thickness of copper wire.

As superhighways develop, personal computers are merging telephone, television, fax, and answering machine into one. These may end up being just a stylish box with no keyboard or mouse, but with the ability to respond to voice commands. Such computers will need to be very powerful, and soon the first of a new breed of optical computers will be needed. The processing rate of today's computers is limited by the speed at which electric currents move inside the circuits. Compared to the speed of light this is a slow crawl, so computers that use lasers to carry their signals will be as far in advance of present-day machines as these are ahead of mechanical calculators.

An unusual future use for the laser was suggested in 1994—using a superhigh-power device to propel a tiny space probe to the stars. According to an American scientist, the laser could accelerate such a craft (using advanced techniques to make it little bigger than a dinner plate) to about 30 percent of light speed in just a few weeks. This would allow a fly-by of Alpha Centauri, the nearest star system, to be made in a little more than a dozen years. The laser would orbit in space and focus on the probe during the acceleration phase like a narrow-beam searchlight. Once the craft reaches cruise speed, the laser could be switched off.

◀ The scene is near-Earth space in the year 2025, as the star probe *Micro Explorer* starts its maiden voyage into the unknown. The destination for the tiny craft is the triple-star system of Alpha Centauri, 4.3 light-years away.

CHRONOLOGY OF ADVANCE

Here are some of the people whose science discoveries, inventions, and improvements have brought about the world of today.

Euclid Greek mathematician (working about 330-260 B.C.). Explained the basic law of refraction. His book *The Elements* laid the groundwork for the mathematics of geometry.

Ptolemy (Claudius Ptolemaeus) Greek astronomer from Alexandria (A.D. 90-168). Tabulated precise measurements of the angles of incidence (when a light ray hits a surface) and refraction.

Alhazen (Abu 'Ali al-Hasan ibn al-Haytham) Arab physicist and mathematician (965-1039). Did further work on the law of reflection and studied spherical mirrors. He was an expert on optics and showed that eyes are receivers of light, gathering light rays from external objects, rather than transmitters of light.

Roger Bacon English monk and philosopher (c. 1220-92). Bacon is credited with the discovery of the glass mirror, eyeglasses, and the magnifying glass. Known as Doctor Mirabilis (the knowledge wizard), he became a Franciscan friar in 1257.

Franciscus Maurolycus (Francisco Maurolico) (1494-1579). Published a theory of lenses in eyeglasses, and how they could cure near- and farsightedness. Compared the lens in the eye to a glass lens.

Hans Lippershey Dutch optician (1570-1619). Invented the first refracting telescope in 1608.

Galileo Galilei Italian mathematician and astronomer (1564-1642). Laid the foundations for modern science by relying on experimentation. Studied motion and used mathematics to establish scientific truths. In optics, he built the first powerful telescope, using it to study the moon, planets, and stars.

Zacharias Janssen Dutch optician (1588-c. 1631). Invented the microscope around 1590.

Willebrord Snell Dutch astronomer and mathematician (1591-1626). Measured the amount a light beam bends when it travels from one substance to another. This is known as the refractive index.

René Descartes French philosopher and mathematician (1596-1650). Using geometric drawings, he described scientifically how the eye focuses.

Francesco Maria Grimaldi Italian scientist (1618-63). Discovered interference patterns and diffraction of light waves, convincing evidence that light is a wave phenomenon. Little attention was paid to this until his ideas were rediscovered in 1803 by Thomas Young.

N. Cassegrain French inventor (born 1625). Designed the reflecting telescope named after him.

Christiaan Huygens Dutch physicist and astronomer (1629-95). An expert on grinding and polishing glass to make lenses, telescopes, and eyeglasses, he believed that light was carried in an invisible substance called ether. He extended the wave theory of light and discovered polarization.

Antonie van Leeuwenhoek Dutch microscopist (1632-1723). Perfected the simple microscope and used it to study many aspects of nature.

Robert Hooke English physicist (1635-1703). Curator of Experiments for the Royal Society, Hooke observed the diffraction effect and studied colored interference patterns. He drew minutely detailed illustrations of his observations made through a microscope and published them in his book *Micrographia*.

Isaac Newton English physicist (1642-1727). Laid the foundations for modern physics by discovering laws of gravity and so showing how the universe is held together. In the field of optics, Newton carried out famous experiments with glass prisms showing that sunlight is composed of separate colors.

Ole Christensen Romer Danish astronomer (1644-1710). Measured the speed of light, calculating it as 133,000 miles per second.

Joseph-Nicéphore Niepce French inventor (1765 1833). In 1822, using silver chloride, he produced the first positive image that could be called a photograph.

Thomas Young English physicist (1773-1829). Established the wave theory of light and the principle of interference. He put forward the theory that all colors are mixtures of three basic colors: red, yellow, and blue. His study of the way light strikes the eye shows how we focus by changing the shape of the lens. He was the first to describe astigmatism of the eye.

Etienne-Louis Malus French engineer (1775-1812). Discovered that reflected light is polarized and called this effect polarization.

Augustin-Jean Fresnel French physicist (1788-1827). Worked on the wave theory of light, showing that light waves are more like three-dimensional water waves than sound waves. He invented the ridged Fresnel lens, which is used in lighthouses to concentrate light.

Louis Daguerre French inventor (1789-1851). In 1839 he announced a process for making photographs using mercury vapor and a sensitized, silvered plate. These became known as daguerreotypes.

William Henry Fox Talbot British inventor (1800-77). Invented the first practical process that used a negative to make a positive print.

Eadweard Muybridge British photographic pioneer (1830-1904). Invented one of the first camera shutters and is best known for his work in capturing movement on film.

Thomas Alva Edison American inventor (1847-1931). Together with his assistant W.K.L. Dickson he invented the Kinetoscope. He also invented the lightbulb, the phonograph, and the first telegraph transmitter and receiver.

▲ George Eastman

George Eastman American inventor (1854-1932). Developed flexible roll film for both still and movie cameras. In 1892 he founded the Kodak company and pioneered cheap, easy photography for all.

Albert Michelson American physicist (1852-1931). Worked with E. W. Morley in 1887 on various experiments to detect the motion of Earth through ether.

Auguste and Louis-Jean Lumière French inventors (1862-1954 and 1864-1948). On December 28, 1895, the Lumière brothers showed their first motion picture films in Paris, the world's first public movie show.

Albert Einstein German-American physicist (1879-1955). Formulated the theory of relativity and changed our ideas of the laws governing the universe. He put them in terms of a universal measuring stick—the speed of light, 186,282 miles per second in a vacuum.

Dennis Gabor Hungarian-British physicist (1900-79). Invented the basic concept of holography, which became a practical means of creating 3-D images after the laser was invented in 1960.

Theodore Maiman American physicist (1927-). The first to generate a laser beam (1960).

Edwin Herbert Land American inventor (1909-). Developed the polarizing filter and the Polaroid instant-developing camera.

GLOSSARY

Achromatic lens A lens that has elements of different types of glass to reduce the problem of chromatic aberration. In this type of lens, a second element corrects the splitting effect of light passing through the first. Modern camera lenses may have up to 20 separate elements to control the light paths and prevent dispersion within the lens grouping.

Additive color mixture Creation of new colors by overlaying beams of colored light. The primary colors are red, green, and blue. When mixed in different proportions, all other colors can be created, including white.

Afterimage A visual sensation that continues for some time after the original light stimulus has stopped. Afterimages may be either positive (when colors and brightness stay the same as the original image) or negative, in which the color and brightness are reversed.

Angle of incidence Angle at which an incoming light ray hits a surface. The angle is measured between the ray and an imaginary line at right angles to the surface. The angle of reflection is the angle at which the ray leaves the surface.

Bifocals A pair of eyeglasses with split lenses. The top part of the lens is ground to correct distance vision, and the bottom to correct close vision.

Binocular vision Seeing with two front-facing eyes, which gives 3-D vision to humans and many other predatory animals.

Blind spot The point where the optic nerves are connected to the brain. There are no rods or cones here, so there is no response to light. The brain "covers up" the spot by filling in the image with images from surrounding areas.

Camera obscura A darkened chamber with an opening that lets in light. Images of the outside world can be projected onto a flat screen inside.

Celluloid A material consisting of cellulose nitrate and camphor, once used for cinematic and photographic film. It has been replaced by cellulose acetate, which does not catch fire. Fire used to be a danger; jammed film

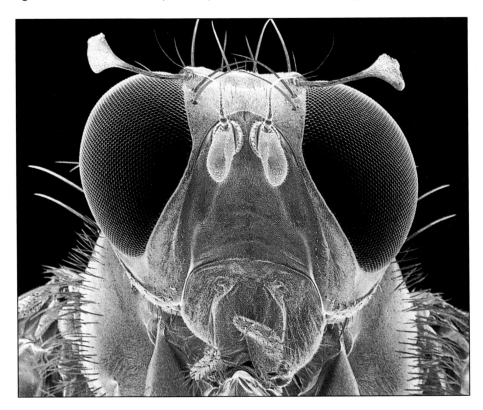

▲ **This startling closeup reveals a fly's compound eye structure.**

in a hot projector housing would ignite.

Chromatic aberration A defect in a lens in which the object in view is surrounded by colored fringes. Aberration is caused by the lens being able to focus only one color correctly. The others are dispersed at different angles, the lens acting like a prism.

Color spectrum The range of visible light. There are no distinct boundaries to colors, but the constituent colors are generally thought of as red, orange, yellow, green, blue, indigo, and violet.

Compound eye Normally found in insects, compound eyes consist of many individual light receptors, each taking in just a small segment of the visual field. Their input is combined into a mosaic image by the insect's brain.

Concave lens A lens that curves inward like a cave or the inside of a bowl.

Cone Cell in the retina of the eye that is sensitive to color and detailed vision. Rods are the cells that take over in dim light, but they do not provide color vision.

Convex lens A lens that curves outward like a ball.

Diffraction The spreading of light as a wave passes an obstacle. *See also* interference.

◀ **The convex front lens of an SLR camera.**

Dispersion Splitting up of white light into a spectrum of different wavelengths or colors. Usually occurs in single or badly designed lenses.

Electromagnetic spectrum Waves of electric and magnetic energy. They move at the speed of light, 186,282 miles/sec in a vacuum. The energy takes many different forms in a range that includes heat energy, gamma rays, radio waves, X rays, and visible light.

Electron microscope A powerful microscope that uses electrons rather than light to produce a magnified image. Electrons have a far smaller wavelength than light and can therefore resolve finer detail.

Epidiascope An optical device for projecting an image onto a screen. It uses a mirror system.

Fiber optic Long, transparent glass or plastic fiber that is used for transmitting light. Such fibers use the principle of total internal reflection—once inside a fiber, a light ray will reflect along the insides until it comes out at the far end.

Focus The point at which rays of light converge or come together. When an image can be seen clearly and distinctly, for example through a camera lens, it is said to be in sharp focus.

Holography A method of producing three-dimensional images by using laser light. The technique involves splitting a laser beam into two beams. The interference caused by the object being photographed is recorded on a photographic plate.

Infrared rays Invisible rays given off by warm objects. We cannot see infrared rays because they are off the visible spectrum, but we can feel them as heat.

Interference The combined effect of overlapping light waves. Where they cross, interference patterns are the result. These can be destructive, resulting in dark lines, or constructive, resulting in bright colors. Such patterns are the cause of many naturally occurring colored effects such as the shimmer of a peacock's feather or the rainbow swirls on soap bubbles. Here, light refracts off the inner and outer surfaces of the bubble; the interference patterns between the sets of light rays cause the surface patterns.

Kinetoscope A nineteenth-century "peep show" that consisted of an upright box with a magnifying lens at the top, through which you could watch a continuous loop of film.

Laser Stands for **L**ight **A**mplification by the **S**timulated **E**mission of **R**adiation. It is a device for producing an intense beam of light waves that are all the same wavelength, all in step, and all parallel.

Lens In the eye; a transparent, oval body behind the iris that changes its shape to adjust the focus for near and far objects. In an optical instrument, a piece of transparent glass, plastic, or crystal with polished surfaces, either concave or convex, through which light can be refracted to enlarge or reduce an image. The shape of the lens looks like a lentil, hence the name, from the Latin word *lente*.

Microscope An optical instrument that magnifies small objects. Microscopes vary from simple (single lens) and compound (multilens) types, to electron microscopes, which illuminate with beams of electrons instead of light.

Objective lens The lens in an optical system (such as a microscope or a telescope) that is nearest to the object being studied.

Optical illusion A picture or scene that tricks the brain into believing a false image is correct.

Optical superhighway Technology that transmits information using fiber optic cables.

Persistence of vision The brief continuation of a visual stimulus after it has ended, a kind of lag effect. It is used as the basis for moving images in the movies and on television.

Photon An elementary particle of light.

Polarized light Light waves that vibrate in a single plane rather than in all directions.

Prism A transparent instrument used for dispersing (breaking up or splitting) light into its components, typically the colors of the rainbow.

◀ **A laser demonstration. This is a fairly low-powered laser, but industrial and military lasers can melt through steel in moments.**

Reflecting telescope An optical instrument that uses a concave mirror to collect light. A lens is then used to magnify the image.

Refracting telescope A telescope that uses lenses to gather light and magnify the image.

Refraction The bending of light as it passes from one transparent medium to another.

Retina Light-sensitive layer that forms the inner lining on the inside of the eye. Light-sensitive rods and cones are contained in the retina.

Scattering Deflection of light by particles, such as the dust in the atmosphere. Blue light is most easily scattered, red the least.

Stereoscopic vision The perception of depth that is achieved by animals that have forward-facing eyes. The overlapping views are combined by the brain for three-dimensional vision. The wider apart the eyes are, the more intense the effect. (Try looking through a pair of powerful binoculars with wide-set front lenses to see this exaggerated effect in action.)

Subtractive color mixture New colors created with paints and pigments; certain parts of the spectrum are absorbed and reflected.

Total internal reflection The principle used in fiber optics and the pentaprisms used in binoculars and some cameras. Light entering such a system reflects off the inside surfaces until it escapes out the far end.

Visible light The small part of the electromagnetic spectrum to which our eyes are sensitive.

Wavelength The distance between crests of a wave. In the visible spectrum, these wavelengths change depending on color: red light has the longest wavelength; violet the shortest.

X rays Long wavelength rays that can pass through human tissue but are stopped by material such as bones and teeth. They are used in hospitals to check on broken bones and by dentists to check the condition of teeth.

FURTHER READING

Ardley, Neil. *Light.* The Way It Works. New York: New Discovery Books, 1992.

Billings, Charlene W. *Lasers: The New Technology of Light.* New York: Facts on File, 1992.

Gardner, Robert. *Experimenting with Light.* Venture Books. New York: Franklin Watts, 1991.

Gardner, Robert. *Optics.* New York: 21st Century Books, 1994.

Hitzeroth, Deborah and Heerboth, Shannon. *Movies: The World on Film.* The Encyclopedia of Discovery and Invention. San Diego: Lucent Books, 1991.

Jay, Michael. *The History of Communications.* Science Discovery. New York: Thomson Learning, 1995.

Lafferty, Peter. *The Inventor Through History.* Journey Through History. New York: Thomson Learning, 1993.

Lampton, Christopher. *Thomas Alva Edison.* North Bellmore, NY: Marshall Cavendish Corp., 1991.

Parker, Steve. *Galileo and the Universe.* Science Discoveries. New York: Chelsea House, 1995.

White, Jr., Laurence B. and Broekel, Ray. *Optical Illusions.* First Books. New York: Franklin Watts, 1986.

MAGAZINES

Petersen's Photographic
Box 50004
Boulder, CO 80323

Popular Mechanics
Box 7170
Red Oak, IA 51591

Popular Science
Box 5100
Harlan, IA 51563

Scientific American
415 Madison Avenue
New York, NY 10017

INDEX